The Orphan Foal

The Orphan Foal

Wendy O'Connor

Cover photography – Jeremy Ricketts

Whorl Publishing Limited
Harraton Lodge, Exning, Newmarket CB8 7HQ, UK
www.whorlpublishing.co.uk

Published by Wendy O'Connor

First published 2018

Disclosure and caution: Every care has been taken to provide accurate information. However, knowledge is not absolute. Management and medical opinions differ. Drugs and nutritional support are subject to change in dosage, formation, etc. The reader is urged to use the information in this book as an adjunct to, and not a substitute for professional veterinary advice, where appropriate, based on a full and proper examination and knowledge of the animal.

ISBN 978-0-9957440-1-1

Typeset and design by Bojangles Design, Newmarket, UK
Printed in UK by Think Ink, c/o Micropress Printers Ltd, Reydon Business Park, Reydon, Suffolk IP18 6SZ

Contents

Supplementary feeding for a foal with a mare

The author

Wendy O'Connor has over 45 years' experience of working with horses, 30 years spent on studfarms and the remaining within the racing industry. Wendy has assisted with hundreds of foalings, most of which have gone very smoothly, resulting in a healthy mare and foal. However, when things have gone wrong, e.g. when the mare rejects her foal, Wendy has developed the skills necessary for caring for the mare and/or foal. Wendy is renowned all over the United Kingdom for fostering and hand-rearing orphan foals and has given lectures on her methods.

The skills Wendy has acquired are passed on in this book. Time is of the essence when things go wrong and this book will be a valuable guide to anyone involved in breeding horses, whether professionally or for pleasure.

For further advice Wendy can be contacted by email - wendy-oconnor@sky.com

This book will be of interest to

- Studfarm managers

- Studfarm assistants

- Studfarm students

- Private horse owners/amateur breeders

- Equine veterinary nurses

- Equine veterinary surgeons

- Equine veterinary students

Foreword

Those of us involved in the breeding of horses are acutely aware of how things can go wrong during foaling or in the neonatal period. The preparation that goes into breeding the mare is immense and is the same for the large commercial stud farms to the single mare owner - from the choosing of the stallion, to the breeding of the mare, the first pregnancy scan, preparing for foaling, the monitoring of the mare until she foals, then there is the foal to consider - standing up, suckling, growing up. At each step having a knowledge and understanding of what is normal and what is not, is essential. Thankfully there are many sources of help for most situations however, managing the orphan foal is not well represented in the educational literature. Although we all hope to avoid having an orphan foal they do arise for a number of reasons: mare death or illness, foal illness, foal rejection, and this is when knowledge and experience on how to manage the situation is essential. It is for these instances that this book has been written. I worked with Wendy O'Connor for 4 years during which time I came to appreciate the science and art behind managing the orphan foal and Wendy and her family had a lot of them to look after! It takes attention to detail, a commitment to feeding the foal correctly and regularly, a need to treat the foal as a horse to avoid humanisation of the foal and an understanding how to foster the foal. Each foal is an individual, each scenario its own but knowing the methods and options that are available allows the best to be made of even the worst situation.

The horse breeding industry will be grateful for this book, even though we all try to prevent problems should they occur the ultimate goal must be to allow the foal to grow-up as a horse and fulfil its potential. This means meeting the foal's nutritional needs but more than that to teach the foal as their mare would have done. There are many ways of doing this but in the heat of the moment they are not always obvious and this reference book is an essential guide to turn to. Each step of the way to 'a well brought up foal' is covered in this book from nutrition and the method of feeding to the fostering process and behavioural needs. Managing the orphan foal is, as with most things in horse breeding, a 'team effort' it is helpful to know there are experienced people out there like Wendy who are willing and able to help those people and their horses when the need arises.

Charles D. Cooke BSc(Hons) BVetMed CertEM(Stud Medicine) MRCVS

Dedication

I would like to dedicate this book to my Dad, Bob.

My Dad knew little about horses, however he did know how to help me reach my full potential, always pushing me even when I was struggling. My Dad was always there to give me words of encouragement and I only wish he could have seen the finished book, I know he would be very proud.

Dad, I love you and thank you.

Wendy x

Acknowledgements

I have had support from many people, especially my daughter Zoe who has been a wonderful 'sounding board' helping with input and advice throughout. Thank you Zoe.

I would also like to thank Charles Cooke MRCVS for his suggestion that I should put my experiences in writing and for the foreword.

Professor Sidney Ricketts FRCVS for reviewing the text and advice on veterinary aspects and additional specialist guidance from Emily Haggett DACVIM, MRCVS.

Whorl Publishing Limited and Jenny Ricketts for producing this book.

Introduction

This book has been written as a practical guide to explain how a foal should be cared for if the dam is unable or unwilling to feed her foal.

- How to foster an orphan foal.

- How to hand-rear an orphan foal.

- How to integrate and educate an orphan foal with other horses.

- How a foal should be cared for if its dam is unable to feed it.

CHAPTER 1

What is an orphan foal?

The standard dictionary definition of an orphan is 'a child whose parents are dead'. In the case of horses, the sire plays no role in the rearing of the foal, so he is not considered when defining the orphan foal and, in certain situations, a foal may be classified as an orphan even if its dam is still alive. For the purposes of this book an orphan foal is one whose dam is dead or cannot or will not provide any/sufficient nourishment for her foal. There are many reasons why this may happen.

You will find, as you read through this book, that it is evident that fostering or hand-rearing an orphan foal is very hard and challenging work. However, it is also very rewarding, especially when you know, that without your intervention, the foal most certainly would have died. As long as the foal is raised as a horse and not as a pet, you will have a very well mannered and socialised horse, which is not 'humanised', and can go on to fulfil its potential whatever that may be.

Fig 1: 'Maggie' a month old orphan foal who has been hand-reared from birth and did well.

How do foals become orphaned?

There are many reasons, as outlined below, why a foal may be orphaned. Some of these problems may result in the mare's death or warrant euthanasia on humane grounds but that is not always the case. Some complications can be treated and the mare saved, although the foal may still need to be managed 'artificially' until the mare has fully recovered. In some cases, an ill or injured mare will lose her milk supply while being treated and she will not be suitable as a mother for that foal.

Complications that will or may result in an orphan foal (by death, euthanasia or incapacity of the dam)

Prefoaling	• Colic • Fracture – serious lower limb injury • Laminitis
During foaling	• Dystocia • Fracture – pelvis or femur • Prolapsed – bladder • Prolapsed – rectum • Septicaemia • Uterine haemorrhage
Post foaling	• Colic • Enteritis • Laminitis • Prolapsed- uterus • Rupture – colon, caecum and peritionitis • Rupture – uterus and peritonitis • Septicaemia • Septic endometritis and laminitis • Severe post-foaling pain • Uterine haemorrhage

If the foal is ill or born prematurely your vet will advise the best action to take.

If the foal is very ill or premature it will almost certainly need intensive nursing in a veterinary hospital (see Fig. 2).

Foal intensive care stables are usually designed to allow the mare to stay near the foal but behind a partition. This allows the foal to be safely and efficiently cared for whilst the mare and foal bond is maintained, in the hope that the foal will be able to feed normally from the mare when it has recovered.

The mare needs to be stripped of her milk regularly, this encourages her to keep producing. It is the old adage 'supply and demand' - the more milk is taken from the mare the more she will produce. The mare's milk can be stored for a few days in a household fridge and given to the foal when it is recovering.

Unfortunately, in spite of one's best attempts, sometimes the mare's milk will still 'dry up' and then there is no alternative but to foster or artificially rear the foal.

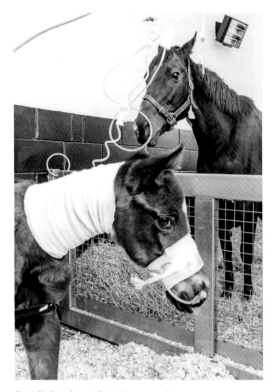

Fig 2: Foal in a hospital intensive care unit.

Very rarely a mare may find the hospital environment stressful and can become aggressive towards handlers and/or her foal. If this occurs, a fostering will need to be arranged for safety reasons.

The following scenarios may occur and/or are important to understand.

If the mare has a serious pre-foaling complication, intervention will only result in the birth of a viable foal if the mare and foal are 'ready for birth' and it is born by emergency surgery, immediately after the mare's euthanasia or by elective Caesarean section.
The mare has other health problems or she is recovering from an illness or surgery.
The mare is aggressive towards the foal and rejects it because: • She has no maternal instinct. (This is rare, although maternal instinct does not always come naturally.) • She has severe post-foaling pain or is feeling ill. • She associates the foal with her pain (e.g. mastitis, sore teats). • She has insufficient or no milk.   These may only be temporary situations.
The mare cannot adequately feed or support her foal because: • She produces insufficient or no milk. • She has severe post-foaling pain or is feeling ill. • She is recovering from an incapacitating illness or surgery. • She has mastitis and therefore her udder is painful. • She stops producing milk due to severe pain or illness. • She stops producing milk because the foal is ill and is not 'sucking'.

What choices do you have?

Depending upon the circumstances, there are three main options:

1. To foster the foal on to another 'nurse' mare.

2. To keep the mare and foal together but hand-rear the foal.

3. To separate mare and foal and hand-rear the foal.

The ideal choice will always be to foster the foal on to another mare. It is the more 'natural' way, and normally works best for the foal's future condition and socialisation. The foal needs the mare for food, affection and its psychological development. Unless you have access to a 'nurse' mare herd, acquiring a foster mare at the right time may be a challenge. Managing the foal until a suitable mare is available depends on age and the circumstances surrounding why the foal was orphaned.

If the mare or foal has died it is best to leave them together for a few hours, as this may help with the 'grieving' process. The survivor may still be upset when finally separated but it seems to accept the situation and comes to terms with its loss better.

The first 24 hours

All newborn foals must drink adequate quantities of their mother's colostrum or good quality donor colostrum ('first milk') within their first 12 hours of life if they are to acquire sufficient antibodies (immunoglobulins) to help fight their inevitable first environmental infectious challenges. Essential antibodies are not transferred across the mare's placenta during pregnancy so foals, unlike many other species, are born without antibodies in their bloodstreams. Therefore, newborn foals are susceptible to infectious bacteria that may invade through the navel, mouth, nose and through any injuries that a foal may sustain.

If the mare has not produced enough colostrum or will not allow the foal to suck, or has a history of producing poor quality colostrum (confirmed by testing with a refractometer - see Fig. 3), or has 'run milk' before foaling, the foal should be given good quality donor colostrum by bottle or stomach tube. As a guide, a refractometer reading (% dissolved solids, i.e. mostly antibodies) of below 20% is poor and donor colostrum should be given. 20-28% is good and above 28% is excellent.

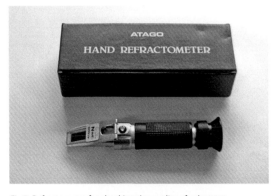

Fig 3: Refractometer for checking the quality of colostrum.

The colostrum (see Fig. 4) should be carefully thawed (warm **not** hot water and **not** using a microwave) from frozen after being milked previously, ideally from a local healthy mare who has produced more than enough colostrum for the needs of her own healthy foal and has never given birth to a haemolytic (jaundiced) foal (neonatal isoerythrolysis). Colostrum should not be used from a mare who has produced a foal with neonatal isoerythrolysis as it may contain antibodies that will harm a foal's red blood cells, producing life-threatening haemolysis (destruction of red blood cells by specific antibodies) and consequential jaundice.

Fig 4: Thawing or warming colostrum, place in a jug of warm water.

When collecting donor colostrum from a recently foaled mare, wait until her foal has had a good suck from one teat and then milk from the other teat into a jug. Transfer the milk into a bottle and once cooled, label and freeze it. If you can get 500 mls that is excellent but any good quality colostrum is worth keeping.

Beware of colostrum substitutes made from cow colostrum which are of dubious immune value for foals.

The mare concentrates high levels of antibodies to the infectious challenges in her environment during the last months of her pregnancy. Therefore, the mother's colostrum is usually the best source for all foals. Even if the mare dies at or around the time of the foal's birth this colostrum should be milked from the mare and given to the foal by bottle and teat or by stomach tube (administered by a vet). Adequate transfer of colostral antibodies can be confirmed by laboratory testing of the foal's blood from 12-48 hours after birth. If, for whatever reason (inadequate colostral immune quantity and/or quality), adequate transfer has not occurred, the foal may be further supplemented by transfusion with commercially sourced hyperimmune equine plasma. Vets look for antibody (IgG) levels in a 24-48 hours old foal's blood of at least over 4g/l and ideally over 8g/l and will recommend transfusion on the basis of considering both the test result and the foal's environmental risk status. If the foal must be moved to another location for fostering or hand-rearing, or the mare and foal must be relocated for the mare to visit a stallion, a prior plasma transfusion may be a wise precaution. Veterinary supervision of newborn foals, whether apparently normal or 'at risk', is highly recommended as this is a critical time. Any poor managerial decisions made at this stage may have unfortunate consequences later.

It is the quantity as well as the quality of the colostrum that can give a foal a good blood IgG level and hopefully prevent the need for a plasma transfusion to be given. Colostrum also appears to have a useful laxative effect on the foal.

The foal slowly loses or uses (fighting infection) the antibodies from the mare's or donor's colostrum over a matter of weeks, by which time the foal's own developing immune system takes over their production.

For a foal that needs to be reared artificially, once it has received colostrum, orphan foal formula (equine substitute) milk can then be fed.

It is recommended that you feed one of the specifically formulated equine milk substitutes available on the market through your local equine feed suppliers. It is advisable to feed mare milk substitutes diluted with more water than the manufacturers recommend until it is clear that the foal is not becoming dehydrated and constipated. The powdered milk supplement requires storage in a damp free environment.

Although goat's milk has sometimes been used to feed orphan foals, it contains two thirds the sugar content and three times the fat content of mares' milk, so it may cause gastrointestinal upsets.

What signs to look for in a newborn foal

A close check should be kept on the newborn foal's vital signs:

- Heart rate: 60–80 beats per minute while calm and quiet.

- Temperature: 37.5–39°C: newborn foals cannot regulate their temperature efficiently, so if it is very cold put a rug on the foal, but at the same time make sure it does not overheat.

- Breathing: 30 chest movements per minute at rest.

- Colour of the gums and tongue: they should be a healthy pink colour.

- Sleep pattern: newborn foals, with a full stomach, tend to sleep for anything from ½ to 1 hour at a time.

- Passing of meconium (first droppings): these are usually dark in colour, quite voluminous, and are usually cleared from the rectum over a period of a few hours.

- Signs of colic: these most commonly occur at this time caused by meconium retention (delayed or impeded clearance). Symptoms may include tail flagging (persistent swishing), sleeping for short periods, repeatedly visiting the udder but not drinking much milk, walking the box, scrapping the bedding, sweating, rolling, lying on its back, getting up and down and generally showing signs of pain. However, only some of these signs may be shown.

- Dehydration: signs are sunken eyes, dry and tacky gums, small amounts of dark coloured urine passed. Pinching the skin will leave a 'ruck' which is slow to return to normal.

- Teeth grinding: usually a sign of abdominal pain.

- Energy level: when the foal is up and not sucking it should be bright, alert, inquisitive and not lethargic.

- Response to sound and light: reacts appropriately.

- General demeanour: bright and alert.

- Not walking into objects: a sign of normal sight and mentality.

- Good coordination.

- Able to get up and down normally.

- Milk coming back down the nostrils when the foal drinks: this can be a sign of a cleft palate or swallowing abnormality.

- Passing urine: normal newborn foal urine is the colour of very weak tea and the foal should pass a good stream regularly. If the urine is very dark in colour, it may mean that the foal is not getting enough milk to drink and is dehydrated (see above). If the urine is red, this may mean that it contains blood and veterinary attention should be sought, without delay, as this may signify a haemolytic (jaundiced) foal.

- With colts, make sure they are letting down their penis to urinate.

- Some colts take a while to fully let down their penis to urinate and this may cause irritation and secondary infection at the adjacent umbilical stump, which will need veterinary treatment.

- Urine may drip from the umbilical stump (pervious urachus). This should be checked by a vet to make sure that the problem resolves without complications.

- Diarrhoea: most 1 week old foals have soft faeces (or degrees of diarrhoea) when their mothers come into foal heat. Orphan foals on artificial milk substitute should maintain normal faeces. Signs of diarrhoea or constipation may suggest that either more or less dilution of the milk powder is required or, if the foal appears clinically ill, may suggest infection and veterinary attention should be sought.

In general terms the foal should appear normally healthy and happy, recognising and drinking well from the mare. The foal should not be standing around and drinking from the water manger as this may be a sign of illness or discomfort and veterinary attention should be sought.

CHAPTER 2

Fostering a foal

Finding a foster mare

There are three main ways of locating a foster 'nurse' mare:

1. Several organisations supply foster mares for the equine breeding industry. These are normally 'cob type' mares which take well to fostering. The mares from these commercial organisations should have been swabbed for Contagious Equine Metritis and blood tested for Equine Viral Arteritis and Equine Infectious Anaemia before arrival, and so, hopefully will be fit and healthy. It is particularly important that Equine Herpesvirus is ruled out in any potential foster mare that has lost a newborn foal before transporting her for fostering.

    The foster mares' own foals are hand-reared, in a group, and are normally prepared for riding or showing. These foals have a good life and are not compromised by their unusual start.

    It will be necessary to pay a fee for the use of a commercial foster mare. Normally the arrangement is to get the foster mare back in foal, and for the orphan foal owner to pay all the mare's keep fees while she is raising the foster foal.

2. An appeal for a foster mare can be put on social media, your local radio station or in the local paper. Some owners contact the TV racing channels and appeal, while racing is on, for a mare that has just lost her own foal or for a foal who needs a foster mare.

3. Register your requirements with The National Foaling Bank who will get in contact if a suitable mare becomes available. There is a small fee to pay to become a member. Normally, it is not necessary to pay for

the use of these mares, although you will have to pay the keep fees.

Good foster mares are few and far between and Thoroughbreds are less likely to successfully foster another mare's foal than non-Thoroughbreds. However, like most things in life, there are always exceptions to the rules!

Very rarely, you may find a mare that will raise her own foal and an orphan together, but this is very unusual (see Fig. 5).

Fig 5: Foster mare with own foal and orphan foal.

Advantages of a foster mare

- The foal is naturally raised by a mare. In most cases an orphan foal brought up by a foster mare will have better condition and 'social skills' than a hand-reared foal.

- Once the initial fostering is successful it is less time consuming than hand-rearing.

- The foal tends to stay with the mare longer and therefore have access to milk for a longer period of time than it would if it was hand-reared.

Disadvantages of a foster mare

- This can be more expensive than hand-rearing, if using a commercial foster mare.

- The initial fostering may take up to a week of constant supervision.

- At the beginning at least two people will be needed to oversee the fostering.

- Fostering is not always successful, so it can be quite stressful for the owner (handler) and the foal.

- It is usually necessary to manage the foal as an orphan until a suitable foster mare can be found and organised.

- The foster mare and foal do not always appear to have the true close bond of a natural maternal mare and foal. Nevertheless, this may still be better for the future of the foal than becoming 'humanised'.

Fig 6: Bales of straw ready to be used to 'box' foster mare in.

Fig 7: Mare in a metal crush with an opening for the foal to feed.

Fostering methods

The mare

- **Barrier:** start with a barrier, so the mare is kept on one side and the foal the other, e.g.

  - Ten bales of straw: to box the mare in (see Fig. 6).

  - Metal mesh gate: to enclose the mare fully, then the gate can be opened when the foal is fed.

  - Crush: this encloses the mare except for an open area for the foal to reach the udder (see Fig. 7).

The disadvantage of the metal gate and crush is that the foal cannot come into close contact with the mare. If the foal does not learn to respect the mare and, because they cannot touch, the bonding process will take longer. The mare may get upset from being penned in and not being able to sniff the foal.

- **Hay net:** to divert the mare's attention and keep her occupied.

- **Hind leg hobbles:** may prevent a sudden accident (if the mare tries to kick the foal) (see Fig. 8).

- **Two ropes:** one for tying the mare up and the other for the foal (in case it is necessary to withdraw the foal from the mare quickly).

- **Muzzle:** over the mare's mouth to stop her from biting the foal (see Fig. 10).

- **Nose twitch:** may initially be necessary depending on the mare's temperament (see Fig. 11).

- **Blindfold:** may help initially to prevent the mare from immediately recognising that this is not her foal.

- **Bridle:** for restraint.

- **Chifney:** a severe bit that gives more control and restraint, if needed.

- **Sedation:** arrange for your vet to sedate the mare before the first introduction. If you are unable to get a vet in attendance, then administer oral sedation by mouth with veterinary advice.

- **Milk supply:** depending on the length of time since the foster mare has foaled (but **not** if she is already back in foal), the vet may wish to give her an injection of prostaglandin. Prostaglandin not only often helps milk supply/let down but also appears to aid the maternal instinct in some cases. This relatively new treatment has been found to help, but only if the timing and protocol is correct, so consult your vet.

Fig 8: Hobbles   Fig 9: Lunge rein   Fig 10: Muzzle   Fig 11: Twitch

The foal

The following are various methods advocated by experienced handlers who claim success - however see below for Wendy's methods.

- Skinning the foster mare's dead foal and tying the skin onto the orphan foal. This is clearly a health challenge for the orphan foal and is now rarely undertaken.

- If available, rub the mare's placenta (afterbirth) over the foal. This may help to encourage the mare to 'think' it is her own foal.

- Rub the mare's sweat and milk over the orphan foal.

- Rub the mare's urine and/or faeces over the orphan foal (less successful and probably unnecessary).

- Apply a pungent nasal decongestant into the mare's nostrils (e.g. Vicks). This will confuse her sense of smell and is more hygienic for the foal than the historic methods detailed above.

However, Wendy uses and recommends the following methods:

1. Start with a hungry foal and a willing mare.

2. Approximately 10 bales of straw. Straw is advised because it gives more flexibility for moving around and is easier than crushes and gates.

3. Two ropes, one for tying the mare up (do not use a chain) and one if the foal requires restraint or needs to be pulled out of harm's way quickly.

4. Hay net and water bucket.

5. Hind hobbles and a muzzle (although the muzzle will be rarely necessary, one should be kept handy).

6. Sedation paste for the mare (as advised and supplied by your vet).

7. The mare's sweat and milk may be helpful.

8. Plenty of patience and a good supply of coffee for the attendants!

9. Someone to assist you.

How to get started

1. Put the foal into the stable where it is to be fostered. The foal can then become accustomed to its new surroundings, feel at ease and put its scent around the stable.

2. When the mare arrives put her into a separate stable and arrange for the vet to sedate her.

3. Move the foal into another stable while you prepare the mare in the fostering stable.

4. Once the mare is sedated tie her up with a rope or have another reliable attendant hold her with a bridle. Put the hobbles (see Fig. 12) on her hind legs and the bales of straw around her. Where you position the mare will depend entirely on the individual stable, but she needs to be tied up or reliably restrained so you can work on her nearside. If possible, tie her up or have her restrained so she is along a straight wall with her hindquarters against a wall in a corner. Remember the mare needs to be able to reach her water bucket and hay net. Position the bales of straw around her, with some in front so she cannot move forward or strike out, some at her hindquarters (nearside) so she cannot swing her hindquarters out or kick the foal, then some by her shoulder so she cannot move out sideways. She needs to be enclosed but with access for the foal to get to the udder and to allow the foal to rub upsides her.

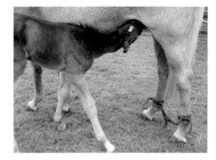
Fig 12: A mare with hobbles on with orphan foal.

5. Bring the foal into the box, talking to the mare all the time.

6. Position the foal so it can find the mare's udder.

7. Encourage the foal to latch on to the teat and drink from the mare.

8. By now the mare is probably sweating due to the action of the sedative. At this time the mare's sweat and milk can be rubbed all over the foal to help mask the foal's own scent.

9. Rub your hands all over the foal; then rub your hands on the mare's muzzle, again getting her used to the scent of the foal.

10. At first do not let the mare look at the foal or try to touch it.

11. Gradually the mare will start to relax and show signs of accepting the foal.

12. Get the foal to rub upsides the mare, so she feels it.

13. It may be necessary to re-sedate the mare, so assess her and ask advice from your vet (different sedatives act for varying time periods).

14. Let the mare and foal guide you as to how quickly to move on from one step to another. You must be flexible. What may work with one mare and foal, might not necessarily work with another. This is something learnt with experience, it is not something that can be learnt from a book!

15. Let the mare smell the foal's hindquarters, but do not let them touch noses.

16. If it looks as if the mare might be aggressive with her teeth, muzzle the mare.

17. If the mare is showing signs of accepting the foal some of the bales can be gradually moved away. However, keep the bales in the stable, just in case the situation changes.

18. Don't be afraid to go back again to an earlier step. It is better to be sure.

19. When the time is right, remove all the straw away from the mare but leave the mare tied up with the hobbles on. The bales can then be gradually taken away.

20. Remember, all mares (natural mothers) will at times lift a leg or nip the foal's hindquarters. This is all part of the education process for the foal to learn who is boss, and it helps with bonding.

21. The foal must learn to respect the mare (she is not just a food source for the foal to use when it suits).

22. Initially still hold the mare on a loose rope, then after about 1/2 hour as long as she is behaving well with the foal, let her loose but still continue to watch them both very carefully.

23. Eventually, the mare can be untied but leave the hind leg hobbles in place.

24. As soon as the mare and foal appear comfortable together take them out into a small paddock or barn area while still holding the mare on a rope. The mare should

still be hobbled at this stage. This will help with the bonding process. A small grass paddock is ideal, the mare will be happy to eat grass, (which will help with her milk supply) and the foal can have some exercise. After a while if they appear happy together you can let the mare loose, while continuing to watch them carefully.

25. As time progresses the strap between the hobbles can be loosened one or two holes at a time, each day. Once the middle strap is removed leave the hobbles on for a further 24 hours. The hobbles can be taken off completely when you are sure that they are no longer needed.

26. If you have had to use a muzzle and the mare still appears aggressive, do not worry about leaving it on (providing she can drink through the holes), although it must be taken off for attended eating. As time goes by there will hopefully be periods when she is less aggressive. This is usually when she is out in the paddock grazing and then you can start to remove it, until eventually it can be left off completely. This type of mare will need continual supervision until you are 100% satisfied she has accepted the foal.

Hopefully, then you have success!

Wendy's top tips for success

- Make sure the foal has not been fed for a while before you start, i.e. it must be hungry. It depends on the age but foals less than 2 weeks old can be left a couple of hours before introducing them. Older foals can be left about 3 hours. When the foal first arrives (if the foal comes to your mare) enquire when it last drank so you know how long it can safely go without food.

- If the foal has never drunk from a mare before you will need to show it where the udder is and encourage it latch on to the teat. You can start by trying to squirt milk into the foal's mouth taking care to avoid aspiration pneumonia (see Page 25). This is one of those times when you will need a lot of patience. If the foal has only ever drunk from a bucket or has done so for a long time and won't latch on to the teat, try feeding it from a bottle to get the suck reflex going (see Page 21). Once it has learnt to latch on and suck from the bottle progress to the mare's teat.

- Always put foals on a one week course of equine probiotic paste. This is because the trauma of losing their dam, the stress of the fostering and the change in diet may cause digestive upsets and probiotics may help.

- Some mares do not like having too many bales of straw around them and will try to jump out, so be flexible to individual needs.

- Each fostering is different - there are no hard and fast rules.

- Work with the mare and foal as individuals, until you understand their likes and dislikes.

- The fostering process may take anything from a couple of hours to over a week.

- Normally an experienced handler can assess whether the process is going to work or not.

- It sometimes helps to try taking the foal away from the mare after a couple of hours and watch her reaction to see if she misses the foal. If she whinnies and looks for the foal you are 'onto a winner'. Do not despair if she doesn't, there is still plenty of time.

- Not all attempts at fostering work.

- Always have a supply of formula (equine substitute) milk available in case the mare's milk supply is inadequate and the foal needs to be supplemented.

- If the mare has a poor milk supply, supplement her feed with cocoa powder (from the local shop). Make sure it is full strength cocoa powder and not low calorie or drinking chocolate. Mix 4 tablespoons of powder with her night feed. Start with 1 spoonful then build up as she gets used to the taste. Your vet may also advise treating her with Domperidone (an anti-sickness medication that has a side effect of usually stimulating milk supply) and she should be fed plenty of fresh cut grass. Your vet may also suggest using prostaglandin if the mare is **not** pregnant again (see page 14) which is a relatively new protocol and can give good results. These methods will hopefully encourage the mare to produce more milk so if contemplating these forms of treatment, consult your vet.

- Any change in a foal's diet can cause it to scour.

- Anti-diarrhoea preventive medicine and probiotics may be advisable until recovered.

CHAPTER 3

Hand-rearing a foal

Hand-rearing a foal, when required, can be very rewarding but it is not easy. It is very hard work, time consuming, and one must be prepared to dedicate 3-4 months of time, energy and patience.

Methods

1. **Bucket feeding** (Fig. 13): foals should be taught to drink from a jug or feed scoop first. As they become confident and drink more, then progress to a bucket. This method is safer and easier than bottle feeding (see below).

2. **Bottle feeding** (Fig. 14): feeding foals from a bottle requires great care by the handler to avoid accidental inhalation of milk. However, bottle feeding a newborn foal with colostrum is the most practical method but great care must be taken.

Fig 13: Relaxed foal feeding from a bucket.

Fig 14: Foal feeding from bottle.

Equipment required

In the stable

- Foal rug
- Warm stable with a top door
- Deep bed of straw
- Fresh supply of water
- Hay
- Heat lamp
- Feed manger

Fig 15: Foal rug.

Fig 16: Well bedded down straw stable.

For feeding

- Bottle and lamb's teat for feeding colostrum to a newborn foal (Fig. 17)
- Good quality dam's or donor's colostrum (that has previously been milked from the mother or a donor mare - see Pages 5 & 6)
- Fresh boiled water
- Formula (equine substitute) milk - as mentioned (see Page 7) there are several different equine milk substitutes commercially available and these can be used when necessary for a foal
- One, 1 litre jug
- Two, 2 litre jugs
- Feed scoop

- Hand whisk
- Small 8 litre bucket
- Kettle
- Fridge
- Sterilising tablets (e.g. Milton) for sterilising equipment (Fig. 26)
- Two large dosing syringes
- Electrolyte supplement (rehydration solution)
- A week's supply of a probiotic in a paste form (available in convenient syringes as supplied by your vet)
- Pepto-Bismol (an anti-diarrhoea medicine)
- Tuff Rock (this helps to line the stomach, firm the droppings and hopefully settle diarrhoea)
- Foal creep feed, for older foal
- **And an endless supply of love, patience, dedication and time!**

Fig 17: Lamb's feeding bottle and teat.

Fig 18: Equipment for bucket feeding.

Fig 19: Thawing or warming colostrum.

Preparation of feed

Colostrum (thaw if using frozen colostrum)

- This is best achieved by placing the container of colostrum into a jug of warm, not hot water (37°C).

- **Note:** If the colostrum is thawed too quickly its proteins (antibodies) will be damaged. Regularly shake the colostrum to circulate it in the bottle. When the water in the jug cools, change it for some more warm water.

- **Do not thaw by microwave** as essential proteins (antibodies) will be destroyed.

- If using fresh colostrum, it can be warmed in the same way as when thawing (see above).

Formula (equine substitute) milk

- Follow the manufacturer's instructions: make up 1 litre of formula milk with warm, previously boiled water in a plastic jug. The brim of the jug must be wide enough for the foal's muzzle to fit in. Some foals like really warm milk, while others prefer it cooler - you will find this out by trial and error with each individual foal.

- If the foal appears to be getting constipated, with the concentration that is being given, dilute the milk with more boiled and cooled water. When the droppings are back to normal, gradually increase the concentration again, to the recommended strength, so the foal's intestines become accustomed to the change.

Teaching the foal to drink

A foal for hand-rearing should be put into the stable when it arrives, with the top door closed and left for a couple of hours to settle down. To succeed at the start, the foal needs to be very hungry and even then, foals often refuse to drink for what can appear to be quite a long time (sometimes several hours). Older foals tend to be more difficult than younger ones. Check when the foal was last fed as this can help with timing when to start.

It should be remembered that the foal has usually just lost its mother and it may have had a long journey and finds itself in a strange place. Not surprisingly, it will be frightened and upset and although the foal is hungry and wants to feed, it may be reticent to do so.

The handler needs to wear protective clothing as the feeding process usually results in the foal liberally splashing milk when its mouth is held near the milk! A lot of time and patience is essential.

From a bottle

- Ideally the foal should be standing to be fed (see Fig. 20) but if it cannot it must be in a sternal position (see Fig. 21) (lying chest, neck and head upright, with its legs folded underneath) or milk will be inhaled (see below).

Fig 20: Feeding from a bottle in a standing position.   Fig 21: Feeding from a bottle in sternal position.

- If the head is held at the wrong angle and the foal does not actually suck, milk can run down the trachea into the foal's lungs causing aspiration pneumonia. This can be fatal if not caught in time and treated as an emergency by a vet.

- The foal's nose should be below its eye level and it should be encouraged to latch on and suck. Feel the throat to make sure it is swallowing – this way you know the foal is drinking.

- As the foal becomes older and drinks more milk, it is more practical to use a bucket.

From a jug/bucket

Older foals will drink from a bucket (see Fig. 23) but when young ones are first learning they usually do not like putting their heads into a bucket. Using a jug or feed scoop is therefore suggested (see Fig. 22).

Fig 22: Foal drinking from a jug.   Fig 23: Foal drinking from a bucket.

25

- Hold the jug (or feed scoop) of milk in one hand, put the other arm over the foal's neck and run a hand down onto the bridge of its muzzle. Put the foal's rear end into a corner of the stable, so it cannot run backwards!

- Try and put the foal's muzzle into the jug of milk (as shown in Fig. 24).

- With a hand on the foal's muzzle, slip a finger into its mouth and open it (so it can 'taste' the milk) (see Fig. 22)..

- Once the foal has got the taste of the milk you are halfway there!

- Keep putting the foal's open mouth into the milk - eventually it will learn how to suck up the milk properly. As with bottle feeding, put a hand on the foal's throat to feel that it is swallowing the milk.

- Some foals begin by lapping (like a dog) but in time they learn to suck and drink properly. Do not worry if the foal puts its whole nose into the milk, this is how some learn to drink. To get a foal drinking properly can take anything from a couple of hours to a couple of days to achieve.

- Orphan foals love contact, so even when they have learnt to drink, still keep an arm over their neck, when they are young. This gives them added reassurance and it is like them leaning up against their mother (see Fig. 25).

- Once the foal is confident with drinking, rotate which side you stand. This helps stop the foal from becoming 'one sided' and you can also run your hands over the body and legs. This all helps with the handling and education and they are never too young to learn.

Fig 24: Teaching an orphan foal to drink from a jug - note hand on muzzle.

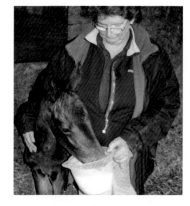

Fig 25: Foal drinking from a jug - note reassuring arm around shoulder.

- Make sure the foal is not getting dehydrated. This can be done by several different methods:

  - **Skin pinch:** pinch the skin and pull it away from the neck and release, then see how quickly it returns to smooth skin. If the skin returns quickly, the foal is normally hydrated but if it takes longer than a few seconds this could mean the onset of dehydration.

  - **Capillary refill:** press (with a fingertip) the foal's gum underneath its lip and release. This will leave a pale area, which should return to a normal pink colour within 1-2 seconds.

  - **Gums:** should always be a healthy pink colour and quite moist.

  - **Eyes:** should fill the eye sockets normally and not appear sunken.

  - **Urine:** the colour of the urine should be like very weak tea not dark and syrupy.

- Small quantities of milk can be gently syringed into the foal's mouth but this must be done very carefully and the foal must swallow because if the milk goes into the foal's lungs it will cause aspiration pneumonia. If dehydration is suspected, an oral electrolyte supplement should be given. Ask your vet for advice.

If you are not making progress and the foal is becoming dehydrated, your vet will need to pass a stomach tube and administer milk directly into the foal's stomach.

Younger foals tend to be a little easier to work with but they can become dehydrated more quickly so it is important to monitor them very carefully.

- Keep a written record of everything the foal drinks, i.e. date, time and quantity.

- Do not worry if the foal does not always drink the amount you expect in one feed. Monitor how much it is drinking over a 24 hour period, and as long as that is within the normal parameters (see Page 29) then everything is fine.

- Any leftover milk can be stored in a jug in the fridge, then topped up for the next feed. With each feed always use the old milk first, so you do not get any wastage. If the milk is more than 48 hours old throw it away and start afresh.

- All equipment must be kept very clean. Remember, it is the same as having a newborn baby. Bottles and teats need to be sterilised (e.g. Milton) and the jugs, whisk and buckets washed in hot soapy water then rinsed (Fig. 26).

As the foal gets older and drinks more you can progress to a bucket. Start by tilting it at a slight angle so it is not so far for the foal to go for the milk, then the bucket can be gradually straightened (see Fig. 23).

You can now start standing in front of the foal instead of beside it, this will help minimise any 'humanising', then progress to holding the bucket over the stable door and finally feed from a manger or bucket in the stable (see Fig. 27).

Fig 26: Bottle brush & Milton for cleaning bottles.   Fig 27: Bucket/manger.

How much and how often to feed?

- The guide is for a Thoroughbred foal, so alter the amounts depending on the breed of horse or pony you are raising (see Page 29).

- Remember that foals less than 2 weeks old prefer warm milk (body temperature).

- If the handler is unable to feed the foal as outlined above, once it is drinking well (and over 2 weeks of age), the bucket/manger (Fig. 27) can be hung in the stable and enough milk poured in for a 12 hour period, so that the foal can drink (ad libitum) at will.

- After 2 weeks of age you can start to build up to the above process but be very careful the foal is still drinking the correct amount.

- This will, of course, only work if the foal is in a stable alone, as its intake must be

Suggested feeding regime for a Thoroughbred foal

Adjust depending on breed of horse or pony.

Age	Milk/food	Quantity over a 24 hour period	How often
Newborn up to 24 hours old	Good quality colostrum and then milk	500ml 11 – 13 litres	Every hour, with a 4 hour break overnight.
Newborn to 1 week old	Milk Hay Fresh water	11 – 13 litres Ad-lib Ad-lib	Every hour, with a 4 hour break over night.
	Probiotics	1 dose	Once a day for a week.
1 to 2 weeks old	Milk Foal creep feed Hay Fresh water	13 – 15 litres 1⁄4 kg, ad-lib Ad-lib Ad-lib	Every 2 hours, with a 6 hour break over night.
2 to 3 weeks old	Milk Foal creep feed Hay Fresh water	15 – 17 litres 1⁄4 kg, ad-lib Ad-lib Ad-lib	Every 2 hours, with a 6 hour break over night.
3 to 4 weeks old	Milk Foal creep feed Hay Fresh water	17 – 18 litres 1⁄2 kg, ad-lib Ad-lib Ad-lib	Every 3 hours, with a 6 hour break over night.
4 to 5 weeks old	Milk Foal creep feed Hay Fresh water	18 – 19 litres 1⁄2 kg ad-lib Ad-lib Ad-lib	Every 3-4 hours, with a 6 hour break overnight. A total of 6 feeds a day.
5 to 6 weeks old	Milk Foal creep feed Hay Fresh water	17 – 18 litres 1-2 kg ad-lib Ad-lib Ad-lib	Every 3-4 hours, with a 6 hour break overnight. A total of 6 feeds a day.
6 to 12 weeks old	The foal will gradually reduce the amount of milk it drinks as it will be eating a lot more hard feed, hay and grass.		Every 4 hours, with an 8 hour break over night.
12 weeks onwards	Start to wean the foal off milk.		

monitored carefully, especially when it is young. It is also very important to make sure that the foal is drinking the milk and not spilling it.

- Clean the bucket/manger thoroughly and throw away any leftover milk every 12 hours.

- The aim is to give the foal enough to last until the next feed but not too much so that milk is left.

- Make sure the foal can reach the water bucket and has hay.

After the age of 2 weeks you can start offering a small amount of foal creep feed. Leave it in a separate manger for the foal to play with and don't forget to refresh it daily. As the foal gets older it will eat the hard feed much quicker so it can then be given as a feed, once a day, at night.

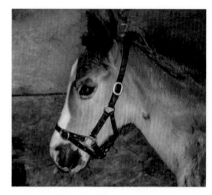

Fig 28: Wearing a head collar helps with education and management.

Always put a head collar (Fig. 28) onto the foal as this makes it easier to handle, although do take it off at night. Putting the head collar on and off helps the foal with the handling and education. Remember to treat an orphan foal as you would any normal foal.

Daily management

Remember that orphan foals can become ill very quickly so you must note any changes and look out for signs that might indicate the start of a problem and the need for veterinary advice. Signs to look out for:

- Not drinking within its normal range
- Not eating
- Very quiet
- Sleeping for lengthy periods
- Standing around the water manger
- Subtle changes of behaviour
- Scouring

- Teeth grinding
- Colic signs
- Discharge from the nose
- Shivering
- Sweating
- Temperature (too high or too low)

If at all concerned, call your vet.

Introducing the orphan foal to the paddock and other foals

Weather permitting, and depending on age, the foal can be turned out into a small nursery paddock for short periods of time every day. Exercise is very important for young foals as it helps them to strengthen and grow in confidence. Even if it is cold, put a rug (Fig. 15) on the foal and turn it out. After several days successfully outside and if the foal is old enough (generally over one week of age), try introducing another foal or companion to help it to socialise.

Teach the foal to lead (Fig. 29) from the start as it makes handling much easier and also teaches the foal respect for the handler from an early age. Handling any foal at a young age is very important but especially an orphan. Start the education as soon as possible and establish boundaries and rules.

Whenever possible arrange for another horse or pony (this can be a mare or gelding, as long as they are of a reliably quiet temperament) or foal, to live with the orphan so it can interact with and learn

Fig 29: Foals should be taught to lead from a young age.

'horse language' and behaviour. Companionship of other orphan foals whilst out in the field is recommended as the foal should learn to play with horses not people. It is very important, if possible, that it has some equine company.

If you do not have a companion for the foal it must go out into the paddock on its own, do not stay in the paddock with the foal as it must learn to be a horse, rather than a 'human'.

When first introducing the orphan foal to its new companion, do not be surprised if it appears frightened and comes running back to you. The foal will still look to you for reassurance and security. Friendship is not instant, it has to build up trust and a bond, which takes time. To begin with, reassure the foal and encourage it to interact with the companion which may initially need to be restrained. Stand by the companion as this will encourage the orphan to come over as it will initially want to be with the human. When you are confident they are getting on well together you can let the companion go, then gradually back away until you can leave the paddock altogether. This can take anything from a couple of hours to a couple of days.

Having a group of orphans, running together, is ideal as they learn from each other and have great fun playing.

If possible, it is advisable to have an older horse or pony to run with them as a role model. An older broodmare either with her own foal or on her own is best but choose companions carefully. If the older horse is too aggressive it can make the orphan frightened of all horses.

After a couple of weeks, turn the foals out into a larger paddock together with another mare and foal.

As time goes on, introduce some more mares and foals to the paddock but always choose companions carefully.

If other mares and foals are not available, make use of any other suitable horse. Remember that the more interaction the orphan has with different horses the more socialised and normal it will become.

Treat the foal as any other foal, the only difference being, you are supplying the milk by bucket.

Until the orphan is weaned, for convenience, it should go back into its own stable at night, on its own, so it learns to be independent. If it is cold at night and the foal appears cold, i.e. shivering or has very cold ears, especially if it is a younger foal, then it should be rugged and the top door closed. The orphan does not have its mother's body warmth and a young foal cannot regulate its temperature as well as an older foal.

Ideally, there should be another form of ventilation when the top door is shut. If it is freezing, use a heat lamp, although it needs to be positioned lower than a normal lamp in the stable, but not low enough so that the foal can jump and hit it. As the foal gets older (unless it is ill) it should not require a rug or heat lamp.

Orphans are more at ease with people than foals brought up by their mothers, so this can lead to them taking advantage, unless they are correctly handled. Remember you are the food source not the parent!

Although the foal must not become 'humanised' you still have to educate it like any other foal, but that does not mean that you cannot show it affection!

Scouring (diarrhoea)

Most foals will scour at some stage but orphan foals are more prone. Some of the reasons are:

- When a foal's diet changes from mare's milk to formula (equine substitute) milk, digestive disturbance usually occurs.

- Orphan foals may not have had colostrum, so their immunity is low and they are more prone to pick up infections.

- Stress from losing mother.

'Foal heat scour' normally happens to all foals around 8-12 days old. This is when the mare has her first after foaling season (heat period). However, the author has had orphans, that are not with a mare during this period who still scour and she believes that at about 1-2 weeks of age the foal's intestines are maturing and acquiring their normal microbial population which causes them to scour, some worse than others.

When the foal starts to scour (which they almost certainly all do), immediately start it on a course of anti-diarrhoea medication (e.g. Pepto-Bismol and Tuff Rock). Ask your vet's advice on dosage as this will depend on the age and weight of the foal and the severity of the scour. Continue the Pepto-Bismol for an extra day or two after the droppings have returned to normal consistency, as this helps keep the stomach settled and hopefully stops reoccurrence. While the foal is scouring take its temperature every day, as an abnormal temperature can be a pre-warning of something more serious.

Also put it on a week's course of probiotic paste. Even if it only scours for 1 or 2 days, finish the week's course.

If the weather is cold, rug the foal (have at least 1 spare rug so it can be changed - they do get very dirty).

Inform your vet as he or she may wish to check the foal or may only ask for the situation to be monitored as long as he or she is kept informed. A faecal sample for testing may be requested.

While scouring, the foal should be kept segregated (contagious infection may be involved, e.g. Rotavirus), and only turned out (in a separate paddock) if the weather is warm and dry.

If the foal goes off its milk or seems lethargic, take its temperature. A foal's normal temperature is 37–39°C. If the temperature is above or below normal, or you are concerned, do not hesitate to call your vet. Remember, young foals can deteriorate very quickly.

If the foal does not want to drink milk, offer it an electrolyte drink. Foals will often drink an electrolyte drink more readily and this will help to keep it hydrated. Dilute the milk down to half strength until it starts to improve. It is very important to maintain liquid intake to replace extra fluid lost during scouring. Monitor the situation carefully until the foal has stopped scouring.

Weaning the foal

- Around 12 weeks of age, start to wean the orphan foal off milk.

- The foal will have been on 5 feeds a day of milk, plus 2 kg of foal creep feed at night.

- Reduce this to 4 feeds of milk a day, for approximately 5 days.

- If it is coping well, cut it to 3 feeds of milk a day.

- After another 4 to 5 days, reduce to 2 feeds of milk. Start to give the foal 2 kg of foal creep feed in the morning as well. Don't worry as if it hasn't eaten it all before going out, it can finish it when it comes in at night with its evening feed.

- Then finally 1 milk feed a day, at night, after the foal has eaten its evening meal for a few more days.

- The foal can start to live out, weather permitting, when it has finished milk feeds but should still come in twice a day for 2 kg of foal creep feed, morning and evening.

- Bringing the foal into the stable helps to reinforce the teaching of manners and its general education.

- Once again, be guided by the foal; some foals wean off milk a lot easier than others.

- As far as the foal's creep feed, monitor the foal's condition very closely over the next few weeks. Adjust the amount fed according to the foal's condition, i.e. if is putting on too much weight, losing it or staying the same.

- The foal may now only need to be brought in once a day, if it is eating plenty of good grass and doesn't need too much additional feed.

- If the foal is going to be living out with other foals you can use a foal creep feeder and not bring it in at all. If several foals have access to the feeder then it is not possible to monitor the amount consumed by an individual.

However, if you are concerned that a foal is not getting enough feed, then bring it into the stable for its feed so you can monitor an individual's intake.

Wendy's top tips for success

I am a great believer in 'feed as they need' (feeding to maintain optimum condition).

- Start by offering the foal 1 litre of milk; if it drinks this do not be afraid to offer more. If the foal does not drink it all, do not worry as there is always the next feed.

- Foals are like any other baby; at some feeds they are 'starving' whereas at other feeds they appear not very hungry. However, if they are consistently not very hungry they must be checked for ill health.

- As the foal gets older you will discover at what temperature they prefer their milk, some like it warmer than others and some foals will even drink it cold!

- Look at the bigger picture. See what the foal drinks in a day, not each feed.

- Some foals have bigger appetites than others.

- As long as the foal is happy, contented, growing well and putting on condition then normally you are doing it correctly.

- Use the recommended feeding quantities as a guide, not as gospel.

- Remember to carry out a routine worming programme - start at approximately 4-6 weeks of age, depending on the individual wormer and your vet's advice.

- Start a vaccination programme from 4–6 months of age, in consultation with your vet.

CHAPTER 4

Supplementary feeding for a foal with a mare

Why may supplementary feeding be necessary?

This may only be a temporary situation (see Page 4), due to the lack or inadequency of the mare's milk supply, or the mare/foal having an injury, illness or recovering from an operation. This situation is quite demanding for the handler (owner) but at least the foal can usually stay with its mother.

Just as with an orphan foal, teach it to drink from the jug/bucket (see page 21). This can take longer because the mare is there. Persevere and remember this could be the difference between keeping them together and having an orphan to rear. If you are struggling to get the foal to drink from the jug/bucket you can muzzle (see Fig. 30) it so it cannot get any milk from the mare making it hungry and hopefully more willing to take the milk from you.

Fig 30: Foal muzzle

Assess the situation regarding how many feeds need to be given and how much to feed. Remember the foal may still be getting some milk from its mother.

The foal's appetite needs to be satisfied but not completely, as the foal still needs to drink from the mare to stimulate her to produce more milk. Ask your vet for advice if unsure.

Hopefully, you are just taking the pressure off the mare, for a short period of time, until she is well again and able to supply enough milk for her foal.

How long should milk be offered?

This depends on the reasons why the foal's feed is being supplemented. Normally it is necessary to supplement the foal for as long as it takes the mare to start producing enough milk to satisfy it. The foal will gradually start taking less from the bucket, as it gets more from the mare, so start reducing the amount of times milk is offered. Then one day the foal will not be interested in the bucket milk and it is then the right time to stop offering it. Be guided by the foal but not totally, use your own judgement or vet's advice as well.

Does supplementary feeding harm the foal's relationship with the mare?

No but, as with everything, it must be approached sensibly. Remember you are only supplying some extra milk to ease the pressure on the mare and you are not there to interact with the foal. Remember, these foals can become too friendly, so do be very strict.

Postscript

- Foals that have been hand-reared can sometimes still be fostered on to a mare.

- Foals that have only drunk from a bucket and have never suckled from a mare can, with patience, learn to suck and drink.

- If you watch newborn foals with their mothers, the suck reflex is clearly a natural response, but to 'latch on' to the teat and get milk is something they appear to have to learn by trial and error.

- If a maiden mare rejects her first foal it is worth, with experienced handlers, trying again to get her to accept her own foal the next year.

Thoroughbred mares do not normally make good foster mothers but, like with most things in life, there are always the exceptions to the rule.

Good Luck!

Glossary

Aspiration pneumonia:
inflammation of lungs and bronchial tubes caused by inhaling milk and secondary infection

Caesarean section:
surgical removal of foetus under general anaesthetic

Chifney:
bit designed for horses that are difficult to lead, with mouthpiece which loops over horse's tongue and behind the chin

Colic:
pain in the abdomen, most commonly caused in horses by impaction of food materials, gas accumulation or twisted intestines but may originate from any abdominal organ

Colostrum:
first milk containing antibodies produced by the mare

Crush:
for 'penning' mare during fostering process. Straw bales or metal gates can be used

Dam:
mother

Domperidone:
anti-sickness medication to help increase milk supply

Dry up:
when mare has no milk in her udder

Dystocia:
birth difficulty e.g. caused by large or awkwardly positioned foetus, smallness of the maternal pelvis, or by failure of the uterus and cervix to contract and expand normally

Endometritis:
an inflammatory condition of the lining of the uterus, usually associated with infection

Enteritis:
inflamed intestines

Euthanasia:
humanely destroying an animal

Flagging:
tail swishing

Haemolytic anaemia:
relating to or involving the rupture or destruction of red blood cells

Haemorrhage:
bleeding

Hobbles:
leg restraint(s) to stop mare kicking

Immunoglobulins:
antibodies, glycoprotein molecules produced by plasma cells (white blood cells) in response to infectious challenge

Laminitis:
painful foot condition caused by inflamation and/or damage to the hoof laminae

Latch on:
foal attaching and sucking from the teat

Mastitis:
inflamed mammary gland, usually caused by infection

Meconium:
first droppings of the foal, formed after drinking amniotic fluid while in the mare's uterus

Nurse mare:
mare used as foster mother for orphan foal

Placenta:
membranes in which foal develops

Prolapse:
organ in question slips out of place, e.g. mare's uterus, rectum or bladder turns inside out and appears externally, usually after foaling

Rotavirus:
contagious virus that can cause gastroenteritis (inflammation of the stomach and intestines)

Scour:
diarrhoea

Septicaemia:
presence of bacteria in the blood stream, i.e. generalised infection

Strip milk:
hand milking mare's udder

Twitch:
made of rope and wood - used on a horse's top lip to assist restraint

Wean:
when milk is no longer given to foal, i.e. mare and foal are separated or milk feeding is ceased

Index

U

Umbilical stump *9*

Urine *8, 15, 27*

Uterine haemorrhage *2*

V

Vaccination programme *36*

W

Weaning *29, 34*

Worming *36*